doll Boutique

Create glamorous gowns, high-fashion hats, and other little luxuries!

★ American Girl®

Published by American Girl Publishing
Copyright © 2013 American Girl

Questions or comments? Call 1-800-845-0005, visit **americangirl.com**, or write to Customer Service, American Girl, 8400 Fairway Place, Middleton, WI 53562-0497.

Printed in China
14 15 16 17 18 19 20 LEO 10 9 8 7 6 5 4 3

All American Girl marks are trademarks of American Girl.

Editorial Development: Trula Magruder

Art Direction & Design: Lisa Wilber

Production: Paula Moon Bailey, Tami Kepler, Judith Lary, Kristi Tabrizi

Set Photography: Kristin Kurt, Travis Mancl

Craft Stylist: Trula Magruder

Set Stylist: Kim Sphar

Doll Stylists: Jane Amini, Kelly Erickson, Karen Timm

Dear Doll Lover,

Make a bitty boutique stocked with glam gowns and fancy accessories for all your doll's exciting events!

First, design no-sew dresses and doll-sized accessories. Next, set up a shop that's trendy, posh, or glitzy. Then slip in the merchandise, and add the kit's cool decor. Finally, open the store's doors!

Now your doll can try on gorgeous gowns for her gala evenings, pick out pretty purses for her parties, and accessorize her wardrobe with high-fashion hats.

Dolls desire a little luxury on those really special days. Now yours can find one-of-a-kind creations with one-stop shopping!

Your friends at
American Girl

CRAFT WITH CARE!

Keep Your Doll Safe

When creating doll crafts, remember that dyes from ribbons, felt, beads, cords, fabrics, fleece, and other supplies may bleed onto your doll or her clothes and leave permanent stains. To help prevent this, use lighter colors when possible, and check your doll often to make sure the colors aren't transferring to her body, her vinyl, or her clothes. And never get your doll wet! Water and heat greatly increase dye rub-off.

It's Just Pretend

All the doll crafts in this book are for pretend only. So don't bring your doll's fur wrap out in the rain, or expose her outfits to sand, sun, or snow.

Get Help!

When you see this symbol  in the book, it means that you need an adult to help you with all or a part of the craft. ALWAYS ask for help before continuing.

Ask First

If a craft asks you to reuse an old item, such as an old purse or shirt, always ask an adult for permission before you use it. Your parent might still need it, so check first.

Craft Smart

If a craft instruction says "cut," use scissors. If it says "glue," use craft glue or Glue Dots®. And if it says "paint," use a nontoxic acrylic paint. Before you use these supplies, ask an adult to check them over—especially the paints and glues. Some crafting supplies are not safe for kids.

Put Away Crafts and Supplies

When you're not using the crafts or craft supplies, put them up high or store them away from little kids and pets. Toddlers and animals might eat your crafts, break them, or even hurt themselves when playing with them.

Search for Supplies

If you can't find an unusual item, such as a rhinestone belt or sparkly tulle, at a local store, ask an adult to search online.

Store Decor

Design your boutique for the grand opening!

Set the Scene

To make a shop, stand up a large trifold poster board. Leave the board its original color, paint it, or attach the pretty paper from the kit. For hat and purse hooks, glue mini spools to the board. To ring up sales, set up the kit's computer.

Less Is More

Luxury shops often have simple displays. Lay down faux fur for a rug, arrange boxes or jars for display shelves, and hang up signs and posters. Easy and elegant!

Display Dresses

To show off the shop's designer fashions, hang gowns on the kit's dress rack, stack gowns on the shelves, or "hire" doll models to wear them. To fill the shop even more, display the dresses, hats, bags, and shoes that your doll already owns!

petite
utique

Dressing Area

Create a private place for your doll to try on gowns.

dressing room

Set Up a Changing Room

To make a dressing room, fold in one side of a trifold poster board, and add a privacy curtain. To make the curtain, glue ribbon loops to a piece of fabric, and slip the loops on a dowel. Lay the dowel on top of the poster board so that the curtain covers the corner.

Have a Seat

Create a seating area for waiting customers. Add a doll seat. Then make a table by placing the kit's tabletop over a small object, such as a dish or jar. Display one or all of the kit's magazines.

Look in the Mirror

Glue craft mirrors or plastic mirrors in the changing area. Add another mirror inside the dressing room if you like.

Deck the Walls

For inspiration, decorate the walls of your dressing area using the kit's posters and wall art, and accent the curtain with stickers.

Kit Creations

Put your kit's collection to work!

Stick Up a Sign

Attach the kit's signs, posters, and pretty papers to the shop's walls. To rehang the signs, use reusable hanging strips or removable poster putty.

Tag and Bag It

Write the selling price of each gown on one of the kit's tags, and attach it to the dress. Use the kit's shopping bags for sacking up jewelry or other small pieces. To make your own shopping bags, decorate small gift bags with pretty papers, ribbons, and stickers.

Push the Paper

Document sales on the kit's receipt pad. To promote even more sales, pass out the kit's business cards to customers.

Set Up the Computer

To make the computer, follow the instructions on both computer sheets. Fold on the scored lines to make the box and the screen. Glue the bottom of the screen to the bottom of the box so that the screen faces the computer, as shown.

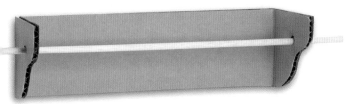

Rig the Rack

Remove the dress rack from the kit, and glue it to the poster-board wall. Let glue set, and then slip a dowel through the prepunched holes.

Design Dazzling Walls

To add pizzazz to the shop's walls, tape the kit's stencil to the poster board, and carefully dab nontoxic acrylic paint over the cut areas with a sponge brush. Let dry, and remove the stencil. For more decoration, press the kit's stickers to the walls or curtain.

Make Money

Punch out the kit's money, store gift cards, and debit cards so that customers can pay for purchases.

Add Nook Necessities

For an accent table, place the kit's tabletop over a cup, box, or other stable object. For magazines, wrap the kit's magazine covers around the kit's cardboard pieces. Attach with glue or double-stick tape.

Light It Up

Give your shop a fancy fixture. Very carefully punch out the chandelier pieces. Perfectly align all three pieces, and then punch a hole in the center ½ inch from the top. Fold each piece in half along its scored line. Run mini Glue Dots along the pointy spine, and press all three spines together so that they touch. Make sure to align the holes at top! Slip string or fishing line through the holes. Lay a dowel across the top edge of the shop's walls, and tie the chandelier to the dowel.

Dress Designer

Create clever gowns with these simple tricks.
Always ask an adult before cutting anything!

Wrap It Up

For a wrap skirt, cut or fold a long fabric strip
that's as wide as you'd like the gown to be long.
Then hold one end of the fabric against your doll's
waist, and wrap the strip around her lower body.
Tuck the other end into her waistband. As you
wrap, pull tightly on the strip or drape it more
loosely to get the fullness you want.

Size a Sleeve

To make floor-length gowns, use long sleeves from
old prewashed clothing. To start, slip your doll—
feet first—up the sleeve to make sure it'll fit her.
If it does, remove your doll, and cut the sleeve
along the armhole seam to give yourself lots of
length. Then embellish the gown with trimmings.

On Again, Off Again

Some dresses can be slipped off the doll and reused. But other dresses you will need to construct on the doll and then take apart when you want to remove them. When fastening the dresses, if you don't want to tie or tuck them in place, try a hair clip, Glue Dots, or closure hooks.

Add Armholes

Try this technique to make an armhole on each side of a shirtsleeve or a leg cut from a pair of leggings or tights. Cut a 1-inch slit 1½ inches from the hemmed or top edge. Slip the dress on the doll, starting at her feet. Remove the dress if you need to trim it.

Do Your Own Tests!

We've tested the materials we've shown on the dolls to make sure the dyes wouldn't rub off onto their vinyl, but you'll use different materials, so review "Craft with Care!" on pages 4 and 5, and check your doll's vinyl often.

13

Lots of Glamour

Design shimmery gowns that light up the night.

Nighttime Knit

Make the fashion world shine with an elegant knitted gown. Slip a sleeve from a metallic knit top on your doll with the cuff at the top. Tie on a belt made from trimmings. For a shrug, cut the matching sleeve in half lengthwise, and tack each half back together along the cut seam with Glue Dots. Slip the sleeves on your doll's arms, and fold over the extra fabric at her shoulder. Decorate with adhesive rhinestones.

Grace in Lace

A lacy gown will enrich any event— from a poetry reading to a formal dinner. Cut sleeves off a lacy blouse, and slip both of them on your doll. Trim off any hemmed edge on the blouse, and cut it into shoulder straps. Tuck the straps into the gown in front and back.

Venetian Velvet

Parade your doll along an Italian piazza in a luxurious velvet dress. Slip a velvet sleeve on your doll. Tuck short tulle strips into the top front edge of the dress, tie on coordinating ribbons, and attach an adhesive bow.

Smooth as Satin

Glam up a gala evening in a creamy satin gown. Cut a satin sleeve from a robe, and slip it on your doll. Use the robe's closure strap for a belt. Attach double ribbon straps to each side with Glue Dots.

Cruise in Blues

Your doll will make a splash in these beautiful blues.

Chic Tunic

Create a twinkling tunic that allows your doll to dash from the pool to the captain's table. Slip a billowy, elastic-cuffed sleeve on your doll, keeping the elastic at the top. Dress up the tunic with a multi-string beaded necklace.

Seagoing Stripes

Set sail in stripes! Cut a white sleeve along the armhole seam, but then cut the angled section of the sleeve straight across, and set it aside. Next, make a straight cut across a striped sleeve so that it is shorter than the white sleeve. Add armholes. Slip both sleeves on your doll—the striped over the white. For a shawl, pull the angled piece over her shoulders, and tuck in the extra fabric. Decorate with star appliqués.

Flower Fringe

Bring your doll ashore in a dress dripping with tropical flowers. Slip a sleeve on your doll, and glue flower appliqués to the bottom edge. (We used a novelty ribboned fabric, allowing us to cut slits into the bottom half before attaching the flowers.) Glue the flowers together into a strap, and attach the strap from the front of the dress to the back as shown. Add matching flowers to your doll's hair.

Grand Glam

For the cruise's "formal night," go overboard on elegance! Slip a pleated sleeve on your doll. Tug both sides of the dress into the center of the bodice, and hold them in place with a glittery pin or pinned-on appliqué. Adorn your doll's hair with a matching appliqué.

Pretty and Posh

Wrap your doll in luxurious and elegant evening gowns.

Rose Garden

Your doll will impress in a floral party dress. Cut the skirt off a toddler's party dress, and wrap it around your doll, keeping the ribbon waistband if the dress has one. Tie the skirt on your doll. For a bodice, wrap a long 3-D rose ribbon 3 or 4 times around your doll's chest. Make shoulder straps from beaded trimmings.

Golden Girl

Bring glitz and glimmer to your doll's fanciest party. Wrap your doll in a long strip of gold lamé fabric. For the bodice, hold a coordinating fuzzy scarf at your doll's waist, and wrap it up around her bodice and each arm before tucking in the end in back.

Princess in Pink

Your doll will look like royalty wearing layers of shimmering sheer fabric. Slip a lacy pink dress cut from a legging on your doll. Then wrap a long strip of sparkly pink fabric around the legging. Use sparkly sheer ribbon for the shoulder straps and bodice ribbon.

Summer Sequins

Don't skip sequins at a summer formal! Slip a girl's drawstring mini skirt on your doll, and pull the strings as tightly as you can. Hold the buckle of a sequined belt in back, wrap the belt around her chest twice, and then slip the end through the buckle. Attach rhinestones to a ribbon strip, and slip it under the belt at the top.

Uptown Browns

Chic and sophisticated—
these gowns suit the city.

Downtown Brown

Your doll will look pert wearing paisley.
Cut the sleeve off a man's cuffed paisley
shirt, make armholes at the cut end, and
slip the sleeve on your doll. For a pretty
top, cut the cuff off the other sleeve,
position it so that the buttonholes are
in back, and add armholes. Slip the cuff
over the dress, and fold down the top
edge. Tie a ribbon through the buttonholes in back to cinch the cuff in place.

Cosmopoli-Tan

Slip a sleek maxi on your doll for gallery
openings and urban events. Cut the feet
off a pair of brown knee-high socks. Make
armholes and a V-neck at the cut end of
one sock, and slip it on your doll. Cut a slit
up to the elastic band of the second sock.
Slip that sock over the first one so that
the band is at the waist and the slit is in
front. Trim with decorative ribbon.

Capital Cocoa and Cream

Take a soft chic dress for a stroll on city streets. First, cut the finger pocket off just one of a pair of extra-long, cream mitten-gloves. Next, cut the fingers—but not the thumbs—off both mittens. Then, slip both mittens on your doll so that the one with the pocket is on top, the pocket is facing front, and both thumbs are at the top. Finally, tie the thumbs in back, slip a cocoa-colored ribbon through the pocket, and tie it in back.

Urban Umber

Design a wild outfit for your doll to wear prowling the plazas. Ask an adult to help you cut the top off a fur boot. Separate the suede from the fur, and trim both pieces into rectangles. Slip a shirt on your doll. Wrap the suede on for a skirt, and pin or clip it in back. Cut armholes in the fur, and slip it on for a vest. Decorate with the boot's buckle accents.

21

Splashy Skirts

Your doll will stand out in these stunning skirts.

Lotta Layers

Your doll will be all the rage in this retro ruffled skirt. Ask an adult to cut a slit up the back and along the bottom of a cotton ruffled handbag, keeping the purse strap intact if possible. Put a shirt on your doll, and slip on the bag skirt. Wrap the purse strap around your doll's waist to hold the skirt closed, and pin it in back if needed. Decorate with shiny 3-D heart stickers.

Sassy Chenille

Show off your doll's spirited side in a lovably "loopy" skirt. Slip a tight-fitting sleeve dress on your doll. Glue a beaded ribbon to the neckline. Then hold one end of a chenille scarf at her waist in back, and tightly wrap the scarf in rows until you reach her ankles. Tuck in both ends. Attach a ribbon bow to one shoulder.

Jazzy Jam

Capture the spectacle of Mardi Gras in a purple beaded skirt. Put your doll in a shimmering dress made from a legging. Slip lots of Mardi Gras-style beaded necklaces on a ribbon, and tie it around your doll's waist. Cut the necklace loops at the bottom, and space beads out.

Black Beauty

Onlookers will sigh at the sight of this densely beaded skirt. First, slip your doll in a dress cut from a legging, and make shoulder straps from beaded trimming. Accessorize with adhesive rhinestones if you like. Next, ask an adult to cut the handle off an old beaded clutch bag and cut a slit along the bottom of the bag. Then slip your doll into the bag, pulling it up to her waist. Gather and pin extra fabric in back. Add a ribbon bow at the waist.

23

Utterly Unique

Your doll will be all smiles with these exotic styles.

French Art

Design a gown that looks like a Parisian painting. Cut both sleeves off a color-splashed blouse at an angle along the armhole seam. Slip both sleeves on your doll so that the cut sides are at the top and angled in opposite directions. Tie the angled ends behind your doll's neck. Add a ribbon waistband.

African Elegance

Whether dining in Cairo or shopping in Cape Town, your doll will look stunning in a vibrant gown. Cut both sleeves off a colorfully patterned blouse, and slip them on your doll. Roll the top sleeve down to the waist. Cut 2 beaded-ribbon strips for straps. Crisscross and attach the straps in front and back with Glue Dots.

Greek Goddess

All will hail your doll's beauty in a Grecian gown. Cut both the sleeves off a ruffly-cuffed blouse at an angle. Make an armhole at the angled part of each sleeve. Slip the first sleeve on your doll so that the ruffle is at the bottom. Tuck and fold the bodice fabric, and tie a ribbon around it. Slip the second armhole the opposite way. Fold over the extra fabric. Add a ribbon waistband. Cut a ruffle from the blouse, and tie it on as a shawl.

Kimono Cool

Pair gold with gems and your doll will shine like Tokyo neon. Cut a short slit up the front of a gold-accented sleeve. Hem both the slit and sleeve with Glue Dots. Slip the dress on your doll. Attach adhesive-rhinestone strips to gold ribbon strips for shoulder straps. Add a ribbon waistband accented with a gem.

Fancy Hats

For luxurious doll toppers, try these cool showstoppers!

Posh Pillboxes

Create a box hat—literally! Cover the outside of a craft box with double-stick tape, and place the box bottom in the center of a large fabric square. Press the fabric against the sides, tucking the extra fabric inside. Decorate with tulle, a sequined band, or a pretty pin.

Ornamental Open-Top

Turn a stretch-comb headband into an elegant cap. Connect the comb to make a circle. Add a wide ribbon with Glue Dots. Attach rhinestone stickers.

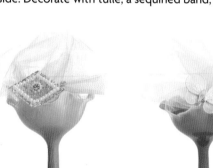

Fluffy Fascinators

Turn tulle, pins, and appliqués into fancy fascinators! Coordinate accents with your doll's outfit, and attach them to a small section of tulle. Attach the fascinator to the side of your doll's hair with a barrette or a bobby pin.

Summer Straw

Create a straw bonnet from a woven place mat! Cut a head hole in the center of the place mat. Decorate the brim of the hat with a 3-D sticker.

Bitty Beret

Fashion a beautiful beret from an old ball-cap! Cut a circle from the top of a baseball cap, and decorate the circle with ribbons. Attach the hat with bobby pins.

Slouchy Skullcap

Cut a sleeve from a stretchy blouse. Turn the sleeve inside out, slip the cuffed end on your doll's head, and tie a knot close to her scalp. Trim off extra fabric, turn the hat right-side out, and add an appliqué.

Tiger Toque

Transform a doll-size sombrero into a winter topper. Cut the brim off a straw hat, dot the hat with glue, and wrap on craft fur. Cover a wooden disk with fur, and glue it on top for a button.

Vintage Veil

Design adorable hats from interesting belts. Cut a belt so that it fits around your doll's head and overlaps slightly. Glue the ends in place. Decorate with tulle and glittery accents.

Brag Bags

Design eye-popping purses from found objects.

Compact Clutch

Close a rhinestone-encrusted compact on a ribbon strip for your doll's perfect glamour purse.

Sparkly Shoulder Bag

Turn a peewee pocket into a shiny shoulder bag. Cut a tiny pocket off an old pair of toddler's pants. For a strap, cut the hem off the bottom of the pants, and glue it to the purse. Glue on beads.

Beaded Handbag

Make a beaded bag from a bouquet wrap (found where wedding supplies are sold). Cut the wrap in half, slip in a folded piece of fabric, and glue the bottom edges together. For straps, glue cord to each side of the bag.

Flashy Pouch

For a faux purse in a flash, slip a decorative lamp pull on your doll's wrist.

Asian Armlet

Close an Asian-inspired coin purse on a ribbon for an evening bag.

Gem Bag

Turn a box into a glitzy purse! Using the technique for the Posh Pillboxes on page 26, cover a cylinder-shaped craft box, but tie the fabric at the top with a cord. Add a ribbon strap. Decorate with rhinestone tape.

Dreamy Drawstrings

Give your doll a working drawstring purse! Trim the sides and bottom of a drawstring gift bag to a size that fits your doll. Seal the seams with Glue Dots. Cut off the bag's original accents, and glue them onto the smaller bag—or add your own decorations!

Glitz and Glamour

Dress your doll for a special event.

Celebrate your doll's special days with her most glamorous look. Create an updo for her hair that finishes with a flashy barrette. Slip her in a dazzling floor-length dress and shiny shoes. Add gemstone jewelry and a gem-covered purse. Finish with a sparkling tulle-tufted cap. Then get set for the oohs and aahs from admirers.

Share Your Style!

Snap a picture of your doll's favorite boutique gown, and send it to us at:

Doll Boutique Editor
American Girl
8400 Fairway Place
Middleton, WI 53562

(All comments and suggestions received by American Girl may be used without compensation or acknowledgment. Sorry, but photos can't be returned.)

Here are some other American Girl books you might like:

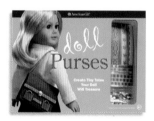